DISTRIBUTED BY

HAL•LEONARD
CORPORATION
WINONA, MN 55987   MILWAUKEE, WI 53213

POLYGRAM MUSIC PUBLISHING

EXCLUSIVE DISTRIBUTORS:
MUSIC SALES LIMITED
8/9 FRITH STREET,
LONDON W1V 5TZ,
ENGLAND.

MUSIC SALES PTY LIMITED
120 ROTHSCHILD AVENUE
ROSEBERY, NSW 2018,
AUSTRALIA.

ORDER NO. AM952633
ISBN 0-7119-7135-8
THIS BOOK © COPYRIGHT 1998
BY POLYGRAM MUSIC PUBLISHING.

VISIT THE INTERNET MUSIC SHOP AT
HTTP://WWW.MUSICSALES.CO.UK

BOOK DESIGN BY
MICHAEL BELL DESIGN.

PRINTED IN THE UNITED KINGDOM BY
PRINTWISE (HAVERHILL) LIMITED,
HAVERHILL, SUFFOLK.

YOUR GUARANTEE OF QUALITY
AS PUBLISHERS, WE STRIVE TO
PRODUCE EVERY BOOK TO THE
HIGHEST COMMERCIAL STANDARDS.
THE BOOK HAS BEEN CAREFULLY
DESIGNED TO MINIMISE AWKWARD
PAGE TURNS AND TO MAKE PLAYING
FROM IT A REAL PLEASURE.
PARTICULAR CARE HAS BEEN
GIVEN TO SPECIFYING ACID-FREE,
NEUTRAL-SIZED PAPER MADE
FROM PULPS WHICH HAVE NOT BEEN
ELEMENTAL CHLORINE BLEACHED.
THIS PULP IS FROM FARMED
SUSTAINABLE FORESTS AND
WAS PRODUCED WITH SPECIAL
REGARD FOR THE ENVIRONMENT.
THROUGHOUT, THE PRINTING AND
BINDING HAVE BEEN PLANNED TO
ENSURE A STURDY, ATTRACTIVE
PUBLICATION WHICH SHOULD
GIVE YEARS OF ENJOYMENT.
IF YOUR COPY FAILS TO MEET
OUR HIGH STANDARDS, PLEASE
INFORM US AND WE WILL GLADLY
REPLACE IT.

MUSIC SALES' COMPLETE
CATALOGUE DESCRIBES THOUSANDS
OF TITLES AND IS AVAILABLE IN
FULL COLOUR SECTIONS BY SUBJECT,
DIRECT FROM MUSIC SALES LIMITED.
PLEASE STATE YOUR AREAS OF
INTEREST AND SEND A CHEQUE/
POSTAL ORDER FOR £1.50 FOR
POSTAGE TO: MUSIC SALES LIMITED,
NEWMARKET ROAD, BURY ST. EDMUNDS,
SUFFOLK IP33 3YB.

HOPELESSLY ADDICTED

MUSIC BY THE CORRS, OLIVER LEIBER & JOHN SHANKS
WORDS BY ANDREA CORR & OLIVER LEIBER

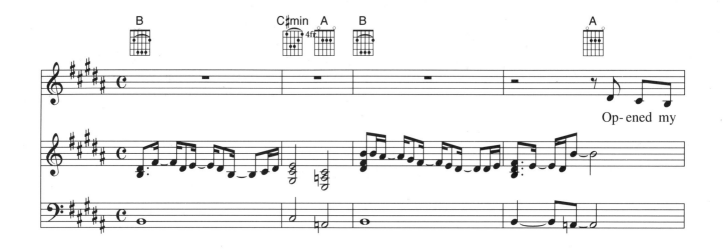

Op-ened my

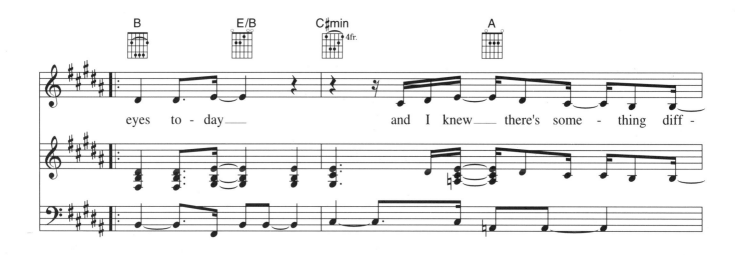

eyes to-day___ and I knew___ there's some-thing diff-

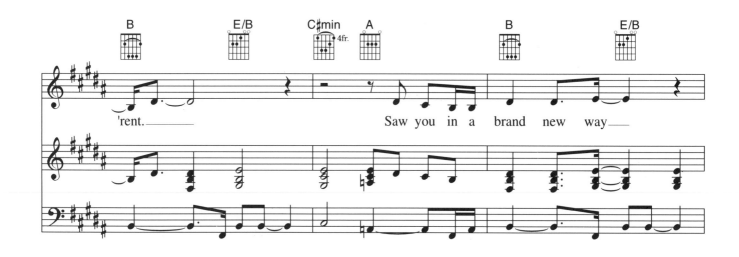

'rent.___ Saw you in a brand new way___

but sudd-en-ly___ I'm fall - ing,___

Was I so blind_____ I was

lo - ving you all___ the___ time___ Now I'm hope - less - ly___ a - ddict-

ed Help-less-ly___ a-ttract - ed. (I'll make a)___

6

7

I'll make a wish this day
And I'll send it to the heavens
That we will always stay
Entwined like this forever
And though the world may change
Coz nothing stays the same
I know we will survive

FORGIVEN, NOT FORGOTTEN

WORDS & MUSIC BY JIM CORR, SHARON CORR, CAROLINE CORR & ANDREA CORR

1. All a-lone,___ star-ing on,___ watch-ing___ her life go___ by.___
(Verse 2 see block lyric)

___ When her days___ are grey and her nights___ are___ black,___

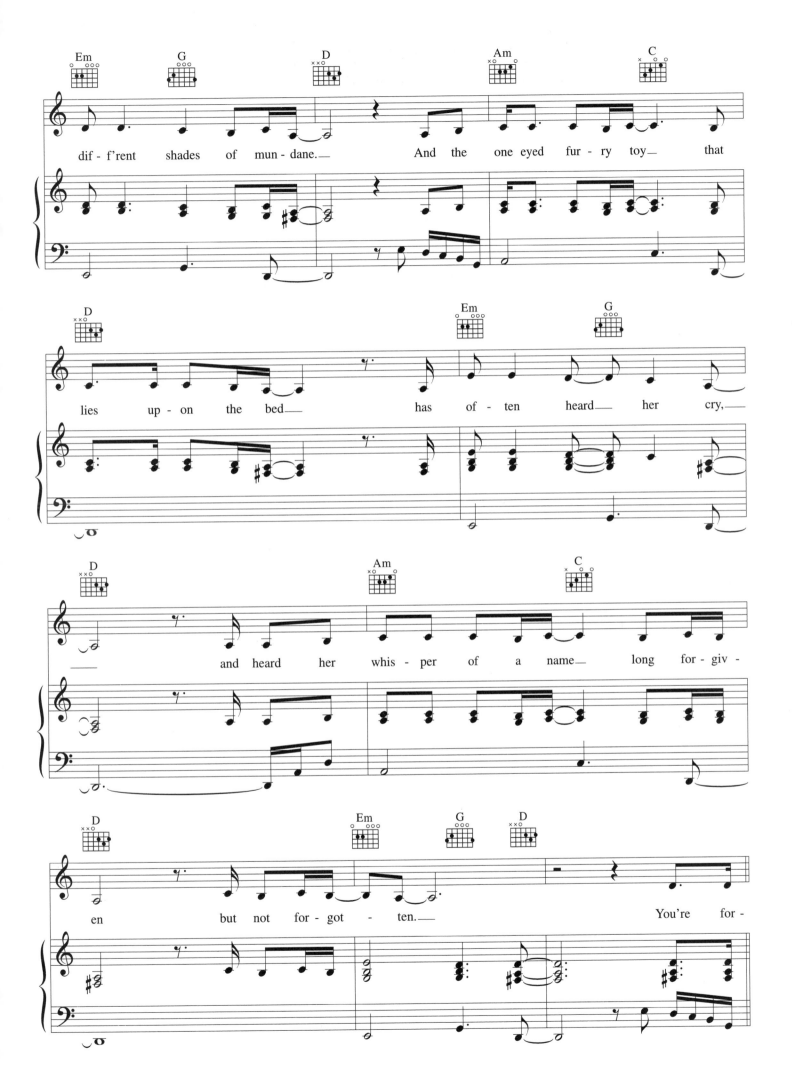

giv - en____ not for - got - ten,____ you're for - giv - en____ not for - got -

- ten,____ you're for - giv - en____ not for - got -

- ten, you're not for - got - ten.____

Still a - lone,_____ star - ing on,

wish - ing____ her life good - bye.____ As she goes search - ing for a man____ long for - giv -

en but not for - got - ten. You're for -

Verse 2:

A bleeding heart torn apart, left on an icy bed
In a room where they once lay face to face
Nothing could get in the way
But now the memories of a man are haunting her day
And the craving never fades
She's still dreaming of a man long forgiven, but not forgotten…

❖ I NEVER LOVED YOU ANYWAY ❖

MUSIC BY THE CORRS & CAROLE BAYER SAGER
WORDS BY ANDREA CORR

an-y-way_____ No I did-n't love you an-y-way_____

I ne-ver rea-lly loved you an-y-way_____ I'm— so

glad you're mo - ving a-way._____

Yeah I am.

Valentino, I don't think so
You watching MTV while I lie dreaming in a MT bed
And come to think of it I was misled
My flat, my food, my everything
And thoughts inside my head.

Before I go I must remember
To have a quiet word to that girl
Does she know you're not a spender
Well I just have to say:

(I never really loved you anyway)

LOVE TO LOVE YOU

WORDS & MUSIC BY JIM CORR, SHARON CORR, CAROLINE CORR & ANDREA CORR

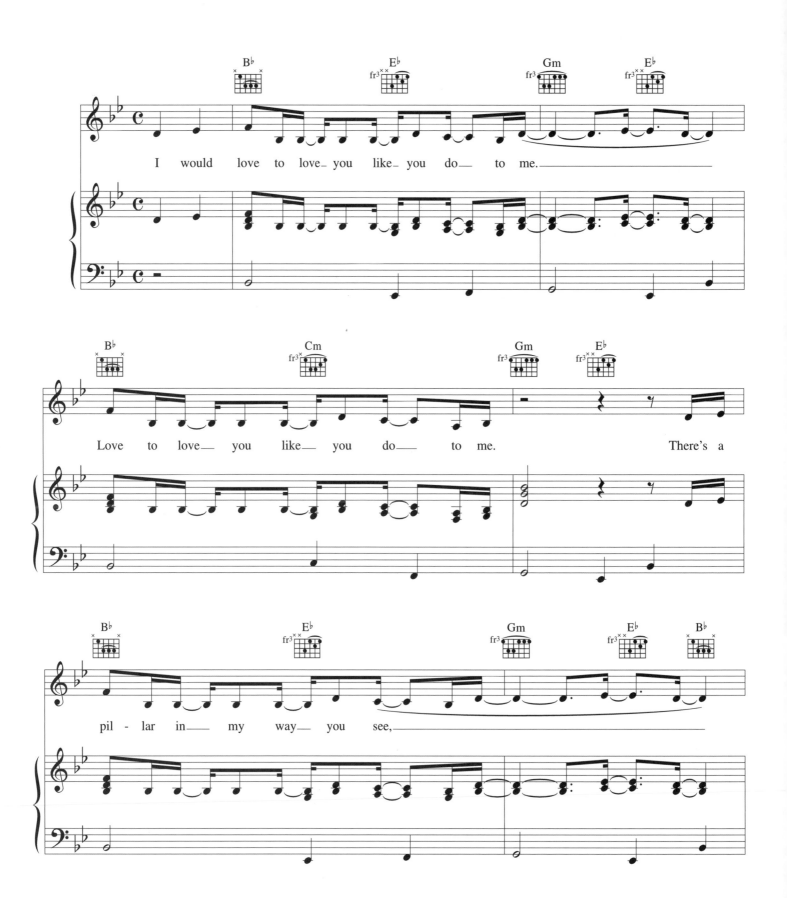

I would love to love you like you do to me.

Love to love you like you do to me. There's a

pil - lar in my way you see,

Though you must leave me, be-lieve me when I tell you I would

love to love you like you do to me.

Love to love you like you do to me. There's a

pil-lar in my way you see,

23

Verse 2:
You recognised my barrier to love
I know there's nothing worse than unrequited love.
I prayed to God that I could give the love you gave to me
But something's lying in my way
Preventing it to be.

ONLY WHEN I SLEEP

MUSIC BY THE CORRS, OLIVER LEIBER, PAUL PETERSON & JOHN SHANKS
WORDS BY ANDREA CORR

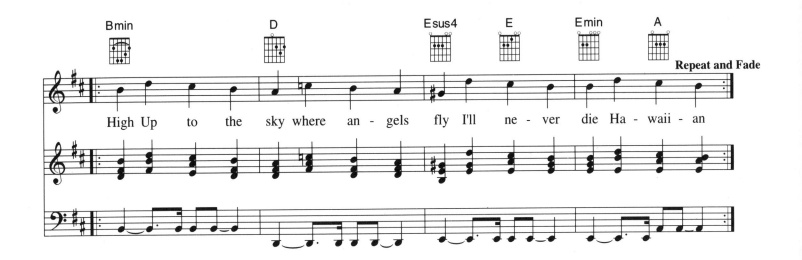

High Up to the sky where an-gels fly I'll ne-ver die Ha-waii-an

And when I wake from slumber
Your shadow's disappeared
Your breath is just a sea mist
Surrounding my body
I'm working through the daytime
But when it's time to rest
I'm lying in my bed
Listening to my breath
Falling from the edge
But it's only when I sleep.....

❋ RUNAWAY ❋

WORDS & MUSIC BY JIM CORR, SHARON CORR, CAROLINE CORR & ANDREA CORR

Say it's true, there's noth-in' ___ like ___ me and the you.

Close the door, lay down ___ up - on the floor. And

30

nev - er gon - na _____ stop fall - ing in love _____

with you. _____

you, _____

with

THE RIGHT TIME

WORDS & MUSIC BY JIM CORR, SHARON CORR, CAROLINE CORR & ANDREA CORR

This is the right time, once in a life time.

So I find it hard to sleep, don't you know. The sun is shining in my window, life's in flow.

1. Mak-ing mu-sic in the morn-ing, laugh-ter's
(Verse 2 see block lyric)

light.

Cre-a-ti-vi-ty it touch-es in full

flight. This is the

right   time._____
life   time._____

Once   in___   a
This   is___   the

Repeat and fade

Verse 2:
Keep on going, let's not lose it, feel the flow
Oh, flying free in a fantasy, with you I'll go.

WHAT CAN I DO

MUSIC BY THE CORRS
WORDS BY ANDREA CORR

I have-n't slept__ at all in days__

It's been so long__ since we've talked.

And I have been here ma-ny times

I just don't know what I'm do-ing wrong.

What can I do to make you love me?

What can I do— to make— you care?—————

What can I say— to make— you feel— this?

To Coda

What can I do— to get— you there?————— No more wait-ing

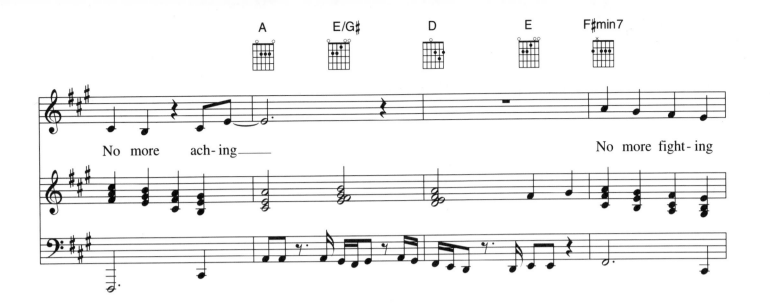

No more ach-ing _____ No more fight-ing

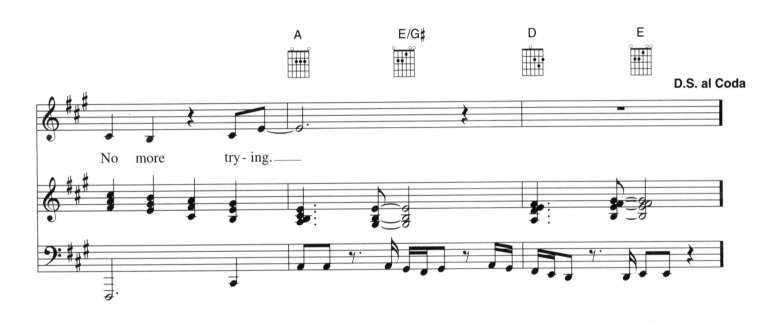

No more try-ing. _____

D.S. al Coda

What can I do _____ to make _____ you love _____ me?

45

What can I do— to make— you care?————————

What can I change—— to make—— you feel—— this?

What can I do—— to get—— you there———— and love——— me?

Repeat and Fade

There's only so much I can take
And I just got to let it go
And who knows I might feel better
If I don't try and I don't hope

What can I do....